THE मन्दीर

AYURVEDIC
COOK BOOK

Ramesh Patel

CURZON ◯

अन्नं ब्रह्म

ANNAM BRAHMA
Food is God

First published in 1997
by Curzon Press Ltd
St. John's Studios
Church Road
Richmond
Surrey TW9 2QA
United Kingdom

© Ramesh Patel 1997

Typeset and designed by Nicholas Awde & Emanuela Losi/Desert♥Hearts
Printed and bound in Great Britain by
T.J. Press, Padstow

British Library Cataloguing in Publication Data
A catalogue record for this book is available from the British Library

Library of Congress in Publication Data
A catalog record for this book has been requested

ISBN 07007 06860 (cloth)
ISBN 07007 06879 (paper)

CONTENTS

आहारशुद्धिवशतः परिशुद्धसत्त्वे
नित्यस्मृतिधरे विकसत्सरोजे
प्रादुर्भवत्यमलतत्त्व विभासिका या
सा त्वं स्तुता गुरुगुह्स्य सावित्री शक्तिः

ĀHĀRASHUDHHIVASHATAH PARISHUDDHASATVE
NITAYASMRUTIDHARE VIKASATSAROJE
PRĀDURBHAVATYAMALATATVA
VIBHĀSIKĀ YĀ SĀ TVAM STUTĀ
GURUGUHASYA SAVITRI SHAKTIHI

Food which among other things promotes joy and
cheerfulness is called **Satvika** because such food
is endowed with goodness and purity.
Therefore it is dear to all good and divine beings.
The Upanishads declare that the purity of the intake
(food) leads to the purity of being whose heart-lotus
opens out steadily to receive and to become the
permanent home of ineffable bliss.
Therein shines the unsullied flame of truth, the power of
Paramatma, and the heart itself becomes guru, the guide.

DEDICATION

I dedicate this book to my wife Usha
and to my parents,
as whatever knowledge and understanding
I have of cooking was given to me by them.
They are excellent cooks in their own right.

आथुर्वेदः अमृताणाम्

ĀYURVEDAH
AMRUTĀNĀM

**Of all nectars
Ayurveda is supreme**

Aum – Pranava – is the root mantra, the soundless sound from which all creation comes. It is spoken at the beginning and end of each sacred verse and each human action. Aum.

ACKNOWLEDGEMENTS

I t was many years ago that I felt the need to write a recipe book with the fundamental understanding of Ayurvedic knowledge, and a number of friends such as Vijay Paul and many of my customers encouraged me to do so. Slowly and steadily I developed the idea until there was a manuscript, which was typed and corrected with great care by Mrs Carol Vijay Paul. So my first heartfelt thanks go to her and all the friends who supported me.

Negotiations began with a number of publishers, but unfortunately I had firm ideas on how the book should be published and none of the publishers could agree with me. Days and years went by, but someone within me was sure that one day I would find the right publisher. It took fifteen years to come to fruition. One evening I was chatting to friends in the restaurant about the book, and our conversation was overheard by Malcolm and Martina Campbell of Curzon Press, who happened to be at the next table. As fans of the Mandeer, they offered to publish my book and let me do it in the way I wanted. The fruit of this long-awaited conjunction is in your hands.

In all our 36 hard working years in the restaurant business, my wife has given her soul to Mandeer's name, fame and achievements and for her help in creating this book I am truly indebted.

Many of our customers have also participated by putting forward suggestions and hints for recipes, and many friends have offered encouragement and help: Mrs Deepa has given help with typing at the last minute; Dr Alpa Bhatt went through and corrected the Ayurvedic section; my revered uncle Shri B. B. Konnur, Shri Priyadarshi Ashoka and Shri Padmakar Mishra provided Sanskrit slokas and translation with calligraphy, and Dr. Jagdish Dave checked and corrected the transliteration; Nicholas Awde typeset and designed the book. I may have forgotten some people, but I am ever so grateful to each and every one of them.

Lastly, I am indebted to all ancient Rushis and writers who have given the knowledge of Ayurveda and words of wisdom for mankind, and to my parents who encouraged me to take an interest in cooking from childhood.

RAMESH PATEL

INTRODUCTION

Ayurvedic food at MANDEER   **Mandeer** is Sanskrit for temple, and the atmosphere in this unique restaurant reflects its name: peaceful, artistic and aesthetically beautiful. Mandeer is the first vegetarian restaurant to have been established outside India and it offers unique Ayurvedic food.

Ayur means life and **Veda** means knowledge or science. This knowledge of life is an age-old science to improve wellness or restore health when there are problems. Ayurveda relies on diet and remedies made from natural herb plants and roots. Although ayurvedic treatments may take longer than others, the results are more permanent and without side effects. Ayurveda is spiritual as it relates the macrocosm of the Universe to the microcosm of the human body. The connection between nature and Self is the foundation for all ayurvedic principles of healing.

The ayurvedic aim of treatments is always to create an equilibrium between the three fundamental forces that control all physical and mental activities. They are reflections of the cosmic

1

forces behind **Creation, Preservation** and **Destruction.**

In today's world, it is imperative to have access to spiritual knowledge and a philosophical framework which can explain health and healing, death and illness as well as global changes which take place ever more quickly. Ayurveda provides us with an ancient system of knowledge that is as valid today as it was originally. At Mandeer, all food is prepared along ayurvedic principles.

About the MANDEER Cookbook

Ayurvedic methods go back thousands of years. You are what you eat, a fact frequently forgotten in the urgency of the modern world, and people look for artificial remedies such as antibiotics when causes and cures are so natural, so obvious and so well proven.

This book takes you back to basics. It does not involve complicated recipes or hours of work. Fast food is available here too, but in an intensely vital and satisfying form. You can discover the simple pleasure of awareness, and appreciate the properties of your ingredients. In time, these things become instinctive.

Intuition, Feeling and Respect

The tradition of Ayurveda provides **balanced cooking**: the balance you want is already there, in the food. You do not need to worry about eating a particular dish for a specific purpose. **Vaghar** is balancing, and as long as you follow the guidelines, the balance will be inherent in the meal and in the body.

The art (not science) of taking the right quantity of any ingredient is something which grows on you. As with putting paint on canvas, you will start with hesitation and become more confident through practice and development of your own judgement. Be guided by natural elements: take everything in the hand or with the fingers to allow the sensation and density of the ingredient to be enjoyed; follow your instinct too when looking at the colour of food. Let your inner consciousness do some decision making.

Touching, in all of life, shows the degree of feeling and closeness. This is a vital part of the relationship you have with the life-giving and health-enhancing food you are going to prepare.

However, do remember that the raw ingredients should not be touched or tasted – the food should be <u>respected</u> once it is cooking. And

3

only when the food has been offered to Agni and other prayers are said should you commence eating.

Chanting and meditating during the preparation of food are valuable – this is the way to remove negative energy and help create balance, which in turn helps to achieve equilibrium in the people eating it. Try to find cooks well-versed in the tradition to give you some experience of chanting, and you may be able to learn and enjoy some yourself.

Symbolizing Hinduism is Vad, the banyan tree. From a single trunk, its branches spread in all directions, giving shade and resting on roots that come from many directions.

4

AYURVEDA

आथुर्वेदः अमृताणाम्

ĀYURVEDAH AMRUTĀNĀM

Of all nectars Ayurveda is supreme.

Ayurveda is the oldest medical system in the world. It dates back to 3000 BC, with its origin in the Indus Valley civilisation of India. It was the first confluence of Aryan and Indian culture.

Ayurveda comes from two Sanskrit words, **Ayur** meaning 'Life' and **Veda** meaning 'Knowledge'. It is usually translated as the 'Science of Life'. The guiding principle of Ayurveda is that the mind influences the body. The state of balanced awareness between body and mind creates a higher state of health and freedom from sickness.

Ayurveda is perhaps the most ancient holistic system of treatment by natural remedies which makes use of the process of nature to restore human beings to a state of balance. It identifies the correct way to live at a given moment to overcome special problems of that particular time or of a particular kind of constitution.

In Ayurveda, as in all Indian philosophical teaching, the universe as macrocosm and man as microcosm are in direct relationship; they reflect one another and one is always present in the other. Ayurveda also has an immediate connection between the use of senses and origin of disease. The Identity (**Samanvaya**) between Nature (**Prakriti**) and the Self (**Purusha**) is the foundation upon which all the principles of Ayurveda are built.

The well-being and the good health of an individual are dependent on the equilibrium of three forces that control all physical and mental activity. These three forces called **Tridoshas** or Humours are a reflection of cosmic forces in microcosmic man. They are in fact a reflection of the Trinity, the principles of creation, preservation and destruction.

These **Tridoshas** — or "three **doshas**" — are called **Vata**, **Pitta** and **Kapha**. They regulate the intricate functioning of the mind-body system with the following functions:

VATA signifies Air. It controls movement and comprehends all the phenomena which come under the function of the central and sympathetic nervous system. To remain alive, the body has to have **Vata** or motion which allows it to breathe,

6

circulate blood, pass food through the digestive tract and send nerve impulses to and from the brain.

PITTA signifies Bile. It controls metabolism. The body has to have **Pitta,** which processes foods, air and water through the entire system.

KAPHA signifies Phlegm. It controls the structure and secondary formation of various preservation fluids. The body has to have **Kapha** to hold the cells together and form muscle, fat, bone and sinew.

These three **doshas** or humours form the tripod of **Ayurveda.** If they are balanced in equal proportions in the body there will be harmony and absence of disease. They keep the physic and the psyche in a healthy condition. This, in essence, is the basic theory of AYURVEDA.

य एव देहस्य समा विवृद्धयै त एव दोषा विषमा वधाय यस्मादतस्ते हितचर्ययैव क्षयाद्विवृद्धेरिव रक्षणीयाः

YA EVA DEHASYA SAMA VIVRUDHHAI
TA EVA DOSHĀ VISHAMĀ VADHĀYĀ
YASMĀDATASTE HITACHARYAYAIVA
KSHAYĀDVIVRUDDHERIVA RAKSHANIYĀHĀ
When the three body elements VATA, PITTA, KAPHA (Air, Fire and Water) are in balance in the body, they promote health. If out of balance, they are extremely harmful. For this reason one must follow the dietary system accordingly to keep the elements in balance.

THE SEATS OF VATA, PITTA & KAPHA

According to
Ayurveda, all illness
can be related to an
imbalance of the
doshas

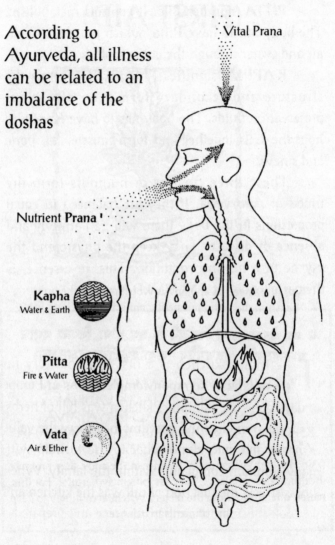

Vital Prana

Nutrient **Prana**

Kapha
Water & Earth

Pitta
Fire & Water

Vata
Air & Ether

8

KITCHEN DOCTOR (FIRST AID)

manjericão

Tusli, the sacred basil plant, is worshipped in the home as
Lakshmi, bringing prosperity, protection and long life.

The Indian kitchen is a first aid repository for
every kind of common complaint. As in Europe
in days gone by, grandma's kitchen was full of herbs,
so in India, mother and grandmother knew the value
of herbs and spices and what to use to help with
many common complaints within the family. When
illness struck, the first port of call was the kitchen and
we took the appropriate herb or spice and prepared a

9

medicine to cure minor problems. Today, we have become so enamoured with modern medicine, not always being cured and often suffering side effects. It is time we learned how to use herbs and spices at home to help family members and through them the whole community . . .

There are many books on Indian cookery. Most of these are written in the time-honoured Western way — "take five cloves" etc. — take a certain quantity of this and a certain quantity of that. But all this is misleading. Indian cookery is something more than a different collection of ingredients and recipes — it is as much a philosophy as the religious scriptures. It is a way of life — the stuff of life itself. Above all, it is an art.

In other arts, like painting and music, there are limits within which the creative artist exercises his own judgement and artistic vision. In Indian classical music, for example, there are many ragas (scale patterns with characteristic rules for their exposition) yet within a set framework a great musician creates new masterpieces, exploring that mystery of life which lies at the heart of music.

Such also is the art of cooking — food is essential to growth, but there is more to its preparation than recipes. In cooking, as in music, there are general rules within which you may express your own creative ability.

Of course you must use ingredients in particular ways, but the choice of foodstuffs, the combination of ingredients and the quantities leave room for individual expression. Use cloves by all means — but not a rigid number. One drop of this, one cup of that, two spoonfuls of something else, will not give you anything more than a mechanical meal. So you will find that the recipes in this book will be only a general guide, to help you discover by trial and error your own way of expressing the art of cooking.

Then there is the very important question of spices. There is a popular misconception that Indian food is simply very hot — many people who try Indian cooking put too much curry powder and red chilli into the food. This is bad from every point of view — flavour, digestion, effect on the body — and even nourishment. When you use the correct spices with the food you achieve harmony instead of discord.

Remember too that every time you cook the 'same' dish the result will be different. The environment, how you feel and even the type of music you are listening to will produce a different result and provide natural change. You will also try different combinations of ingredients, since we always love what is new. In this way the mind will always be happy to receive it and will not get bored with the same thing.

Many beginners use ready-made curry powder or garam masala, and merely mix this with everything they cook. These general purpose powdered spices do not go well with everything. So which spices belong to which foods? For example, there is a bean called papadi — if you merely cook and eat it, it causes wind in the stomach. To counteract this the spice ajwain is used so that the food is balanced. Tradition has systematised the knowledge of which spices belong to which foods, and these classifications will be explained in this book. They will then give a guide to the best and most balanced way of preparing food.

The combination of spices with other ingredients in the preparation of a meal also involves the **vaghar** — a process which nobody who has written on Indian cooking has ever properly explained before. There is a beautiful Gujarati proverb which says: "He whose **vaghar** is not right, his dal (lentil) is not right; and he whose dal is spoilt, so will his whole day be spoilt". (The word 'vaghar' is the key cooking process which will be explained shortly.) The proverb means that if you begin the day by eating wrongly prepared food, the whole day will be ruined. It also implies that without good 'vaghar' the food is not right, either in flavour or effect. As soon as you give vaghar to the food, you know at once what it is you have prepared and that it is going to be very good.

Now there is one other very important question: This is a book about purely vegetarian cooking and people who are unaware of this system find it difficult to understand its traditional basis in India. First of all, it must be quite clear that meat is not necessary for proper nourishment, and those who are sensitive to or disgusted by the preparation of food from dead animals may be sure of perfect nourishment, good health and happiness from a vegetarian diet.

We know that according to Western classification, foods contain different kinds of nourishment — proteins, carbohydrates, fats, vitamins, salts and water. These are all to be found in vegetarian food. But according to Indian philosophy there is another classification which arises from the study of the whole nature of man and his actions.

आयुःसत्त्वबलारोग्यसुखप्रीतिविवर्धनाः
रस्याः स्निग्धाः स्थिरा हृद्या आहाराः
सात्त्विकप्रियाः
कट्वम्ललवणात्युष्णतीक्ष्णरूक्षविदाहिनः
आहारा राजसस्येष्टा दुःखशोकामयप्रदाः
यातयामं गतरसं पूति पर्युषितं च यत्
उच्छिष्टमपि चामेध्यं भोजनं तामसप्रियम्

ĀYUHUSATVABALĀROGYASUKHAPRITIVIVAR-
DHANĀHĀ
RASYĀHĀ SNIGDHĀHĀ STHIRĀ HRUDYĀ
ĀHĀRĀHĀ SĀTVIKAPRIYĀHĀ
KATVAMLALAVANĀTYUSHNATIKSHNA-
RUKSHAVIDĀHINAH
ĀHĀRĀ RĀJASASYESHTĀ
DUHKHSHOKĀMAYAPRADĀHĀ
YĀTAYĀMAM GATARASAM PUTI PARYUSHITAM
CHA YAT
UCHCHHISTAMAPI CHĀMEDHYAM
BHOJANAM TĀMASAPRIYAM

Lord Krishna says to Arjuna: The food which is dear to each
is threefold. Hear the distinctions of these. The foods which
increase vitality, energy, vigour, health and joy and which are
delicious, bland, substantial and agreeable are dear to the pure.
The passionate desire foods that are bitter, sour, saline,
excessively hot, pungent, dry and burning, and which produce
pain, grief and disease. The food which is stale, tasteless,
putrid and rotten, leavings and impure is dear to the Tamasic.
—BHAGAVAD GITA

14

There are three **Gunas** or qualities of life:

Sattwa   Rajas   Tamas
Purity   Passion   Inertia

Different combinations of these qualities are present in everyone, and are responsible for a whole range of character traits. Those in whom there is over-predominance of one quality need to balance this by developing other qualities.

Ultimately one should purify other rajas and tamas by one's actions, particularly in a chosen kind of yoga. But these qualities are also affected by the food which we eat. Fruits and vegetables which have a pure effect without reacting on the system are classified as sattwic. Foods like onions and garlic are rajasic or stimulating. All meat food is regarded as highly tamasic and harmful to all temperaments. If a very rajasic person continues to eat rajasic or over-stimulating food, he will become over-excitable. When a tamasic person keeps to a tamasic diet he becomes lazier and subject to all kinds of illnesses.

The effects of food are subtle, but all food enters into the substance of man and becomes part of him, and the effects are cumulative over a long period of time, affecting not only the character of a person but also his environment.

There are therefore many things to bear in mind — the question of the correct choice of foods for nourishment, the spices which belong naturally to the foods in question, and the qualities of foods and spices. Yet within these, just as within the rules of music and painting, there is tremendous scope for individual expression and creativity. In the same way that ragas are divided into groups with specific qualities associated with emotions, colours and effects on the listener, so the time-honoured ways of Indian cooking allow the cook to be an artist, and to serve others with daily food that will improve their character and life. Cooking is an art and also part of an ethical life. Food should therefore be cooked with reverence, peace and joy and served to everyone with love, care and kindness. As the food is received we should do so with respect and happiness and pray that nowhere on this planet should any creature in air or water go without food or drink.

Trishula is the trident of Shiva, sceptre of the Shaiva Dharma. Carried by yogis, its points represent Ida (Desire), Pingala (Action) and Sushumna (Wisdom), and the three Gunas: Sattwa (Purity), Rajas (Passion) and Tamas (Inertia).

VAGHAR AND MOVAN

Homakunda is the ancient Vedic altar of fire. The Homa flame
represents divine consciousness, through which sacraments are
solemnised and offerings are made to the gods.

In order to achieve the vital balance in the nature
of the product, there are two essential aspects.
Vaghar is the technique of using whole spices
rather than the powdered spices (which for their
part enhance taste and create a soothing effect in the
body); to make the vegetable (or beans) neutralised
so far as air and fire and water is concerned. The
spices differ according to the items being cooked.

17

Movan is a technique where any type of oil or ghee (purified butter) are used, either in dough or liquid dough (such as pancake mix), to ensure the finished item is soft (and remains so).

VAGHAR

The Vaghar is a process during which certain spices, such as mustard seeds, are heated in a small amount of oil or ghee, and are later used to flavour the food. When cooking a vegetable dish the vaghar is prepared before the vegetables are added; when cooking lentils or soups their Vaghar is prepared last. The technique of preparing the Vaghar is the same in all cases, and only the spices may vary.

When preparing a vegetable vaghar, a little oil is heated in a pan large enough to hold all the ingredients and, when the oil is ready, whole methi (fenugreek) and rai (mustard seeds) are added. The mixture will make popping sounds within a few minutes. When the sounds fade add a pinch of hing (asafoetida) powder along with the vegetables, and immediately cover the pan in order to save the aroma. When cooking lentils or soups, the oil is heated in a separate pan and the Vaghar is added to the cooked lentils or soup before the pot is covered with a lid.

18

MOVAN

The process of adding one or two large spoonfuls of oil or ghee to flour before adding water to make a dough or batter is called Movan.

The movan ensures that the finished preparation — chapati, puri, etc. — has the desired softness or crispness, even when it is cold. More ghee or oil added to the flour will make the finished preparation more crisp. The greater the amount of Movan, the more crispy the bread will be.

These two techniques will be mentioned in the recipes in this book in further detail according to the dish. The taste and texture of dishes will depend greatly on the successful use of these techniques. Mastery in these techniques will come with practice.

> When you touch the spices
> your inner consciousness
> will tell you
> how much to put in.

द्वितीय अनुवाक

अन्नाद्वै प्रजाः प्रजायन्ते । याः काश्च पृथिवी꣫श्रिताः ।
अथो अन्नेनैव जीवन्ति । अथैनदपि यन्त्यन्ततः । अन्नꣳहि
भूतानां ज्येष्ठम् । तस्मात्सर्वौषधमुच्यते । सर्वं वै तेꣳन्नमाप्नुवन्ति
येꣳन्नं ब्रह्मोपासते । अन्नꣳहि भूतानां ज्येष्ठम् । तस्मात्सर्वौषधमुच्यते ।
अन्नाद्भूतानि जायन्ते जातान्यन्नेन वर्धन्ते । अद्यतेऽत्ति च
भूतानि । तस्मादन्नं तदुच्यत इति ।

MATTER AND LIFE

ANNĀD VAI PRAJĀH PRAJĀYANTE, YĀH KĀSH
CHA PRTHIVIM SRITĀH, ATHO'ANNENAIVA
JIVANTI, ATHAINADAPI YANTI ANTATAH,
ANNAM HI BHUTĀNĀM JYESTHAM, TASMĀT
SARVAUSADHAM UCHYATE, SARVAM VAI
TE'NNAM ĀPNUVANTI YE'NNAM
BRAHMOPĀSATE, ANNAM HI BHUTĀNĀM
JYESTHAM, TASMĀT SARVAUSADHAM
UCHYATE, ANNĀD BHUTĀNI JĀYANTE, JĀTĀNI
ANNENA VARDHANTE, ADYATE'TTI CHA
BHUTĀNI, TASMĀD ANNAM TAD UCHYATA ITI.

From food, verily, are produced whatsoever creatures dwell on
the earth. Moreover, by food alone they live. And then also
into it they pass at the end. Food, verily, is the eldest born of
beings. Therefore it is called the healing herb of all. Verily,
those who worship Brahman as food obtain all food. For food,
verily, is the eldest born of beings. Therefore it is called the
healing herb for all. From food are beings born. When born
they grow up by food. It is eaten and eats things.
Therefore it is called food.

—BHAGAVAD GITA

CATEGORIES
& PROPERTIES

Chinmudra is the gesture of realisation, reflection and silent teaching. Is is one of the Mudras, the gestures used in sacred dance. These movements of the hand focus the mind and charge the body with spiritual power.

CATEGORIES AND PROPERTIES OF FOOD

Basic Categories

FLOURS

Most people use only wheat flour, but there are so many other flours used in Indian cooking which provide good nutrition such as gram flour, corn flour, millet flour, rice flour, bean flour, and so on . . .

OILS

In India, according to the climate, we use different oils in different parts of the country: coconut oil, peanut oil, mustard oil, sunflower oil and purified butter (ghee). We use mustard and sesame oil mainly in the cold season, whereas in the hot season we use coconut and peanut oil as the effects on the body change according to the weather.

VEGETABLES

India has all types of weather and many different vegetables grow there. India has been vegetarian for many thousands of years, and so much effort has been put into growing a wide variety of vegetables. Now that the world is becoming smaller many of these more exotic vegetables are available in Europe, and it is high time we tried to learn how to cook these vegetables, in the traditional manner. These different types of vegetable are very valuable in helping to maintain our health.

WHEAT

Wheat is a basic food staple in many parts of the world. India has a huge tradition of making many tasty items from wheat and in this chapter we shall explain methods, applications and variations.

RICE

Rice is also a basic food staple in many parts of the world. It has been used for thousands of years in India, and there are many, many dishes which will be explained in this chapter.

BEANS & SPLIT PEAS (DALS)

In Europe many people have no proper idea of the many different types of beans and the ways of cooking them. All grains are called pulses and those beans split in two are called dal. Most whole beans are prepared in a thick form, whereas dals (lentils) are prepared in a soup form and there are many ways of cooking both of these items, which will be described in this chapter.

SAVOURIES

Savouries are prepared from vegetables, beans and various flours, spices, condiments, fried and baked, in many different styles. In India there are thousands of varieties of snacks and savouries.

SWEETS

In every part of the world, desserts are the most popular item at a celebration or festival. In India there are many thousands of different sweets prepared from wheat, rice, beans, and milk. The sweetmeats are prepared for fasting, weddings, birth celebrations and seasonal celebrations, and take into consideration the time of year as well as the health of the people.

YOGHURT

The West has, during the past few decades, awakened to the good health qualities of yoghurt, but in India yoghurt has been used for many thousands of years and is used in desserts, food items, and drinks, and using the by-products of yoghurt, such as buttermilk, cheese, ghee, in cooking.

DRINKS

According to the season, there are many different drinks prepared in India either hot or cold, even according to the time of day — or in illness and good health, there are many different types of drinks. Again, the main purpose is not just to enjoy the drink, but to maintain good health and enjoy!

CHUTNEY & PICKLES

Of all the thousands of pickles and chutneys prepared in India, the main one known in the West is mango chutney. But chutneys and pickles are prepared from many different fruits, berries, herbs, vegetables, etc. Every meal is accompanied by appropriate chutneys and pickles.

Foods according to property

The three body elements — **Vata, Pitta** and **Kapha** (air, fire and water) — when in balance (**Tridosha**) and harmony in the body promote health; if out of balance they are extremely harmful. For this reason one must follow the dietary system accordingly to try to keep the element in balance.

The categories of elements and tastes given on the following pages provide an essential guide to understanding how they can be enhanced or destroyed in different combinations.

QUICKLY DIGESTED FOODS

Ginger, bitter gourd, sucking mango, mangosteen, carrot, rice, buttermilk, pomegranate, parwal, puffed rice, black pepper, masur, white radish, lemon, small aubergines, black salt (sanchal), rock salt (sindaiva), dry ginger, elephant foot (Indian yam), turmeric (haldi), asafoetida (hing), apple, betelnut.

HARD TO DIGEST FOODS

Black gram (urad), chickpea, muth, tamarind, cucumber, Alphonso mango, sliced mango, unripe banana, yellow marrow, dates, wheat, tindoor, black-eye bean, water melon, sesame seed, yoghurt, basundi, black grapes, popcorn, spinach, potatoes, almonds, sweet lemon, large aubergine, butter beans, string beans, sprouted beans (of any kind), dry vegetables, sugar cane juice, apple, betelnut.

KAPHA PRODUCING FOODS

Black gram (urad), tamarind, mango juice, mango fruit, kokkum, sugar, gur (Indian brown sugar, or 'jaggari'), sesame seeds, milk, oranges, string beans, sprouted beans, dry vegetables, sugar cane juice, apples.

PITTA PRODUCING FOODS

Black gram (urad), tamarind, ripe cucumber, kokkum, gur, water melon, sesame seeds, unripe pomegranate, salt, large aubergine, butter beans, sprouted beans, dry vegetables, asafoetida (hing)

VATA PRODUCING FOODS

Alphonso mango, gur (2nd class), rice sesame seeds, spinach, muth, honey, masoor, ripe white radish, beans of all kinds, sprouted beans, dry vegetables.

KAPHA DESTROYING FOODS

Ginger, ripe tamarind, amla, bitter gourd, Alphonso mango, unripe banana, dates, carrots, chickpea, buttermilk, water melon, pomegranate, Indian marrow, parwal, maize, honey, muth, puffed rice, black pepper, masoor, mustard seed, lemon, salt, butter beans, drumstick, rock salt, elephant, food, ginger powder, betelnut, haldi, asafoetida (hing)

PITTA DESTROYING FOODS

Amla, cucumber, bitter gourd, Alphonso mango, mango pulp, unripe banana, yellow pumpkin, wheat, chickpea, milk, coconut, parwal, water, maize, sweet lemon, string beans, apple, drumstick, rock salt, betelnut, haldi.

VATA DESTROYING FOODS

Black gram (urad), fresh ginger, tamarind, amla, mango juice, ripe mango, unripe banana, yellow marrow, dates, sugar, carrot, wheat, tindoor, buttermilk, ripe water melon, yoghurt, pomegranate, milk, black grapes, oranges, coconut, parwal, sliced mango, almonds, fresh butter, salt, lemon, small aubergine, string beans, apple, rock salt, ginger powder, haldi, asafoetida (hing).

FOODS WHICH ARE COLD

Amla, bitter gourd (karela), ripe mango, banana, dates, wheat, tindoor, butter oil (ghee), chickpea, rice, spinach, dals (split beans and peas), black grapes, coconut and coconut water, potatoes, maize, puffed rice, fresh butter, string beans, dry peas, sugar cane juice, apple, rock salt, betelnut.

FOODS WHICH ARE HOT

Fresh ginger, black gram (urad), tamarind, kokkum, carrots, tindoor, ripe melon, sesame seeds and oil, yoghurt, parwal, white radish and its leaves, mustard seeds, salt, aubergine, ginger powder, haldi.

FOODS WHICH INCREASE THE DIGESTIVE POWER

Ginger, tamarind, small round bitter gourd, cucumber, ripe mango, kokkum, buttermilk, sesame seeds, spinach, oranges, coconut water, parwal, fresh butter, lemon, black salt, elephant foot, ginger powder, betelnut, halde, asafoetida (hing).

FOODS WHICH PREPARE STOMACH CONTENTS FOR CORRECT ASSIMILATION

Carrots, turia, parwal, puffed rice, white radish and its leaves, lemon, aubergine, drumsticks, haldi, asafoetida (hing).

FOODS WHICH ARE EASILY DIGESTED AND HELP TO BIND OTHER FOODS IN THE INTESTINES

Ginger, cucumber, Alphonso mango, kokkum, carrot, yoghurt, pomegranate, muth, masoor, ginger powder, all fruits.

FOODS WHICH CAUSE DRYING IN THE BODY

Tamarind, cucumber, Alphonso mango, chickpea, rice spinach, popcorn, potatoes, maize, honey, masoor, ripe radish, dried peas, elephant foot, betelnut, haldi.

STIMULATING FOODS

Black gram (urad), ginger, ripe mango, ripe banana, cabbage, yellow pumpkin, dates, kachadi, basmati rice, jalebi, pomegranate, milk, Indian marrow, black grapes, coconut water, parwal, potatoes, almond, fresh butter, lapsi (cracked wheat), sweet lemon, vada from urad dal, small aubergine, shrikand, sugar cane juice, apple, ginger powder.

FOODS WHICH INCREASE STRENGTH

Black gram (urad), ripe mango, ripe banana, coconut, dates, kachadi, wheat, jalebi, sesame seeds, pomegranate, milk, basundi, potatoes, fresh butter, chapati, lapsi, urad dal vada, string beans.

REJUVENATING FOODS

Amla, ghee, triphala, milk, harade.

LAXATIVE FOODS

Tamarind, gur, wheat, milk, black grapes, black-eye beans, sugar cane juice, harade.

FATTENING FOODS

Yellow pumpkin, ripe banana, sesame oil, basundi, black grapes, chapati, lapsi, urad dal vada, shrikand, sugar cane juice, apple.

FOODS BENEFICIAL TO THE HEART

Ginger, dates, old gur, milk, coconut water, parwal, black salt, ginger powder.

अहं वैश्वानरो भूत्वा प्राणिनां देहमाश्रितः
प्राणापानसमायुक्तः पचाम्यन्नं चतुर्विधम्

AHAM VAISHVĀNARO BHUTVĀ
PRĀNINĀM DEHAM ĀSHRITAH
PRĀNĀPĀNASAMĀYUKTAH
PACHĀMI ANNAM CHATURVIDHAM

Becoming the life of fire in the bodies of living creatures and
mingling with the upward and downward breaths,
I digest the four kinds of food.
—BHAGAVAD GITA

The Konrai blossom symbolizes the grace of Shiva in our life.
Throughout India the plant is praised in his shrines and
temples.

Spices and Condiments

I n Indian cooking, spices, condiments and herbs are used to a greater extent than anywhere else in the world. God has given all these ingredients packed with goodness and if used daily, many common complaints can be prevented and cured.

Herbs and spices are used to balance air, fire and water, while giving us the minerals needed by the body. According to Ayurveda there are six tastes: sweet, sour, bitter, pungent, salty and hot. If all these tastes are used daily in our food many illnesses can be prevented. People sometimes avoid the bitter and pungent tastes of food, and that is why many problems increase later on in life.

Therefore, it is important that we learn to use spices, herbs and condiments properly in our everyday cooking.

SPICES AND CONDIMENTS

	Indian name	English name	Whole or Powder	
1	AJAWAIN	Lovage	✓	–
2	DHANIA	Coriander	✓	✓
3	ELAICHI	Cardamom	✓	✓
4	GARAM MASALA	Ground mixed spices	✓	✓
5	HALDI	Turmeric	✓	–
6	JEERA	Cumin	✓	✓
7	JAVANTRI	Mace	✓	✓
8	JAIFAL	Nutmeg	✓	✓
9	KESAR	Saffron	✓	–
10	KALA JEERA	Onion seed	✓	–
11	KHAS KHAS	Poppy seed	✓	–
12	LAVANG	Cloves	✓	–
13	MERCHI	Chilli	✓	✓
14	METHI	Fenugreek	✓	–
15	MARI	Black Pepper	✓	✓
16	RAI	Mustard seed	✓	–
17	SAVA	Dill seed	✓	–
18	TAJ	Cinnamon stick	✓	✓
19	TIL	Sesame seed	✓	–
20	VARIYALI	Aniseed	✓	–
21	BADIYAN	Star aniseed	✓	✓

Warming/ Cooling to the body	Digestant/ Stimulant	Producing/ Subduing Vata (Air)	Producing/ Subduing Pitta (Fire)	Producing/ Subduing Kapha (Bile)
W	S	S	P	S
W	D/S	–	S	S
C	D	S	P	S
–	–	–	P	S
W	–	S	P	S
W	D/S	S	S	S
W	D/S	–	P	–
W	D	S	S	S
W	D	S	S	S
C	D/S	–	–	–
–	–	S	–	P
W	D/S	S	P	–
W	D	S	P	S
W	D	S	P	S
W	D	S	P	S
W	D	–	S	S
W	D	S	P	S
W	D	S	P	S
W	D	S	P	P
W	D	S	P	S
C	D/S	S	S	S

SPICES AND CONDIMENTS

1. AJWAIN stops hiccoughs and flatulence, and has antiseptic qualities.

2. DHANIA has a very cooling effect in fever.

3. ELAICHI is good for a cough, suppresses vomiting when eaten with banana, and is a good digestive aid.

4. GARAM MASALA enhances the flour of food and helps in digestion.

5. HALDI reduces fat, purifies and circulates blood, enhances the body colour, and works as best antiseptic element.

6. JEERA is very cooling, with a sweet taste.

7. JAVANTRI is rejuvenating, improves appetite and digestion.

8. JAIFAL — as JAVANTRI (7)

9. KESAR — as JAVANTRI (7)

10. KALA JEERA is cooling but with a strong or bitter taste.

. . . as household remedies

11. KHAS KHAS is binding, helpful against diarrhoea.

12. LAVANG is helpful in cough and colds.

13. MERCHI is helpful in digestion, hair growth.

14. METHI is helpful in coughs and colds, as well as joints problems.

15. MARI is good for the heart, increases appetite.

16. RAI kills germs , removes gastric distension.

17. SAVA suppresses hiccoughs, vomiting and painful wind in children.

18. TAJ clears throat, removes thirst, improves appetite.

19. TIL oil thickens and lengthens hair, massaged on gums firms teeth, best for body massage.

20. VARIYALI is useful in reducing fever.

BEANS

When any bean is split it is called **dal**,
e.g. chanadal, mungdal, etc..The general term for
flour made from any bean is **ata**.

Indian name	English name	Whole	or Split
CHANNA	Chickpea	✓	✓
CHOLA	Black-eye bean	✓	–
MUNG	Green garam	✓	✓
MASUR	Red split dal	✓	–
RAJMA	Kidney bean	✓	
VATANA	Soya bean	✓	–
TUVER	Split yellow ochre lentil	✓	–
URAD	Black garam	✓	✓
VAL	Indian 'baked bean'	✓	–

Sprouted	Flour	Comments
✓	✓	Used in too great a quantity will cause wind
–	✓	Cook with a good quantity of oil to reduce wind
✓	✓	Most easily digested of all the beans, produces the least wind
–	✓	Cook with plenty of oil; removes fever
–	–	Very healthy bean, reduces impurity in the blood and imparts strength
–	–	Heavy bean, cook with plenty of oil, very tasty
–	–	Very healthy bean, improves skin texture
–	✓	Rejuvenating, increases weight
✓	✓	Cook with plenty of oil; produces Vatha

41

USEFUL FLOURS

Indian name	English name
BESAN	Gram flour (chickpea)
MAKAI ATA	Maize flour
BAJRI ATA	Millet flour
CHAVAL ATA	Rice flour
GAHU ATA	Wheat flour
URAD ATA	Black gram flour

Comments

Used to make all kinds of bhajias, savouries and snacks, and sweets.

Used to make breads and savoury snacks.

As above; plain and spicey bread.

Used to make dosai, utapa and some sweets.

Used to make breads of all kinds and sweets.

Used to make dosa and (if coarse) sweets, edli, vada, etc.

43

OTHER USEFUL ITEMS IN THE KITCHEN

PAPAD	Papadom
PAPDI	Rice papadom
VADI	Drops of coarsely ground blackeye beans, spiced & sun-dried
LIMDO	Curry leaf
KOTHMIR	Fresh coriander
PHUDINO	Mint
METHI	Fenugreek
ADARAK	Green ginger
KISMIS	Sultana

Crisp wafer prepared from mung or urad flour, plain or spiced, sun-dried

Crisp wafer prepared from rice flour and spices, sun-dried

Crushed various lentils with spices, shaped into small ball, sun-dried

Sweet neem tree leaf used for flavouring

Fresh (dried) coriander leaf used for flavouring and making chutney

Fresh (dried) mint leaf used for flavouring and making chutney

Fresh (or dried) leaf used for flavouring

Fresh ginger root — many uses

Used for sweet dishes

COOKING OILS

Indian name	English name
KOPREL	Coconut
MUNGFALI	Peanut
SARSAV	Mustard
TAL	Sesame
GHEE	Butter
SURAJMUKHI	Sunflower

NOTE

The main cooking oils used in India are those shown above. The use of a particular oil often depends on the weather conditions, as well as economic circumstances.

In Northern India where it is cold, mustard oil is used for its heating qualities; in Central India peanut and sesame oils are used, and in Southern India, where it is very hot,

Comments

Used for cooking mainly in South India.

A very popular oil, but too much use creates wind.

A heating oil, used mainly in Northern India; also used for massage to encourage the fire element.

A popular oil, besides cooking, it is also used for massage, also beneficial to the eyes.

Ghee is the best of the oils and is cooling to the body. It is therefore used extensively in the hotter regions of India, and always for sweets.

A popular oil, creates a lighter style of cooking.

coconut oil is used. Only in the region of Rajasthan is ghee used most often.

Throughout India, ghee is always used in the preparation of sweets. Not only is it the most pleasant tasting of the oils in this respect, but because of its cooling properties it is the one oil which is acceptable to use with milk and sugar, so often the main ingredients of Indian sweets.

47

VEGETABLES

Most of the vegetables listed are available in Indian grocery stores

Indian name	English name
BHINDI	Okra; Ladies Finger
BAIGAN	Egg Plant; Brinjal
CHOLI	Indian Runner Bean
DUDHI	Marrow (White)
KARELA	Bitter Gourd
TINDORA	Soft Mini Cucumber
PARVAL	Hard Mini Cucumber
VATANA	Dry Yellow Peas
SURAN	Elephant's Foot
BATATA	Potato
GAJJAR	Carrot
TURIA	Hard Surfaced Cucumber
GALKA	Soft Surfaced Cucumber
GUVAR	Indian Runner Bean
PAPDI (Valor)	Fresh beans
DUNGRI	Onion
SARAGVO	Drumstick
KORU	Red Pumpkin
KOBI	Cabbage
FULKOBI	Cauliflower

CODES	
C — cumin (jeera)	**H** — hing (asafoetida)
F — fenugreek (methi)	**L** — lovage (ajwain)
G — garlic	**M** — mustard (rai)
	[CFLM = whole seeds]

Air	Fire	Water	VAGHAR
✓	–	–	FMH
–	✓	–	FMH
✓	–	✓	LMG
–	–	✓	FMH
–	✓	–	MH
✓	–	–	FMH
–	–	–	FMH
✓	–	–	FMH
–	✓	–	FMH
✓	✓	–	FMH or CH
–	✓	–	FMH
–	–	✓	FMH
–	–	✓	FMH
✓	–	–	LMG
✓	–	–	LMG
–	✓	–	FMH
–	✓	–	MH
–	–	✓	FMH
✓	–	–	FMH
✓	–	–	FMH

FOOD COMBINING

Helps Digestive System and Balancing of Food

CODE

F — fenugreek (methi)
G — garlic
H — hing (asafoetida)

L — lovage (ajowan)
M — mustard (rai)
[FLM = whole seeds]

Vegetables	Vaghar
Potato and brinjal	FMH
Potato and cabbage	FMH
Potato and cauliflower	FMH
Potato and beans	FMH
Potato and peas	FMH
Potato and okra	FMH
Potato and onion	FMH
Potato and bitter gourd	MH
Dudhi (white marrow) & channa dal	FMH
Turia and mung dal	FMHG
Choli (runner bean) & cucumber	LH
Choli (runner bean) & brinjal	FMH
Choli (runner bean) & turia	FMH
Okra and cucumber	LH
Guvar (runner bean) & red pumpkin	LHG

TASTE (Rasa)	ELEMENT (Dhosha)		
	VATA (Air)	PITTA (Fire)	KAPHA (Water)
Sweet	destroys	destroys	increases
Sour	destroys	increases	increases
Salt	destroys	increases	increases
Bitter	increases	destroys	destroys
Hot	increases	increases	destroys
Pungent	increases	destroys	destroys

MEASUREMENTS

I n India teaspoons, tablespoons, cups, etc., are not used to measure quantities. Simple, straightforward and accurate measurements are made using the hands. For example:

1. A pinch with thumb and first finger is **chapti**
2. A pinch with thumb and first and second fingers is **moti chapti**
3. A fistful is **muthi**
4. An open-handed scoopful is **khobo**

Generally, 1 muthi of rice per person and 1 muthi of flour per person are sufficient.

In this book we provide standard measuring units but we would like you to use our method to learn how to measure instinctively through practice. When cooking for two to three people, the amounts for powdered spices are:

coriander	1 teaspoon	**moti chapti**
cumin	½ teaspoon	**nani chapti**
garam masala	¼ teaspoon	**chapti**

turmeric	¼ teaspoon	**chapti**
chilli	¼ teaspoon (or less)	**chapti**
salt	according to taste	

Of course, these are only extreme generalisations —
experience alone will bring success.

बह्यार्पणं ब्रह्म हविर्ब्रह्याग्नौ ब्रह्मणा हुतम्
ब्रह्मैव तेन गन्तव्यं ब्रह्मकर्मसमाधिना

AUM BRAHMAR PANAM, BRAHMA HAVIH,
BRAHMA AGNU, BRAHMANA HUTAM,
BRAHMAIVATENA GANTAVYAM, BRAHMA
SAMADHINA

O God bless this food so that it brings vitality and energy to
fulfil the mission and serve humanity
O God bless this food so that we remain aware of the within
and the without
O God bless this food so that we love all and exclude none
Bless those who have provided this food, who have prepared
this food and who will eat this food.

TRADITIONS

कठोपनिषद्

ॐ सह नाववतु । सह नौ भुनक्तु । सह वीर्यं करवावहै ।
तेजस्वि नावधीतमस्तु । मा विद्विषावहै ।
ॐ शान्तिः शान्तिः शान्तिः

AUMSAHANĀ VAVTU, SAHANAU BHUNAKTU
SAHA VIRYAM KARAVĀ VAHAI,
TEJASVINA VADHIRTAMASTU, MĀ VIDVISHA
VAHAI AUM SHANTIHI SHANTIHI SHANTIHI.

Let us grow together spiritually in our heart and
grow useful things on this planet. Let us share together
whatever we have achieved. Let us accumulate vigour and
knowledge together and through that let us cross the darkness
to the light together. Let jealousy never come in between us.
Let peace be here, there and everywhere.
—KATHOPNISHAD

There are traditions upon traditions. Every
caste and every creed has its traditions.
Traditions are followed, new ones appear,
old ones are forgotten. There are good and bad
traditions. We do not mind leaving behind the bad,
but when we stop following the good, sometimes

we invite disasters and unhappiness, knowingly and unknowingly, for us and all of society.

There are some universal traditions which, if we all followed them simultaneously, might prove beneficial to all. A perfect example is the offerings which are performed in India before eating.

First of all the meal is prepared with joy and love in a clean atmosphere, without touching or even taking the aroma of the food, as these are both Apavitra (spiritually diluted) so we cannot offer it to anybody — and certainly not to God or the Deities. When the food is prepared, you offer it first to Agni (Fire) as he is responsible for cooking your meal. If the god is pleased, he will shower his blessings upon you and your food.

Secondly, offer the food to Gai (Cow) as she gives milk, butter and butter milk to sustain our body and vigour. If she is happy, she will bless and give more milk with happiness.

Thirdly, to Kutro (Dog) as he is the one who is most faithful and obedient to you and your neighbours, who looks after any newcomers and gives warning day and night of intruders so that you may avoid theft or harm.

Fourth, to Pakshi (Birds), as they are around you every day bringing joy and music in Nature and helpful in many ways in the environment. If they are content, they will do the job in Nature and the environment which you do not see or understand.

Fifth, to any unfortunate human being — poor or old, priest or neighbour. You must feed them, so that they also bless you and you have the satisfaction of doing something good and they in return pray and bless you, and happiness will be showered upon you.

Lastly, just before you start eating, you must pray and offer the food mentally with meditation to all your kith and kin, elders, friends and also those who have departed and live in the Astral World.

All these have deep and scientific values. For example, from time to time we hear that people have eaten poisoned food and as a consequence they die suddenly. But if you first offer the food when it is ready to the fire, the change in colour of the flames will show you of any change in the food. The aroma of the burning food will also indicate any problem and then you are forewarned. Likewise, the Bird, the Dog and the Cow will give you indication of unfortunate happenings so that you will not eat bad food. The Dog is particularly very careful in what he eats, as he always smells the food first and if there is anything amiss, he will avoid it.

Before the meal you should also repeat the sloka given at the beginning of this chapter, as the whole world has become self-centred: if we do not care for others, nobody will care for us, but if we all care for each other, then there will be less misfortune, misunderstanding and society will grow with care, love and peace. So we invite everybody to share our food.

In India food is traditionally eaten by hand. Nowadays we increasingly eat while walking, talking — even in our beds. All this is bad, since when we eat we do not concentrate on the reason or purpose of eating the food. The purpose of eating is to digest the food and it should assimilate in the body to give you strength and vigour. Instead the the manner in which we eat today does not do this and we have the consequences of being ill and unhealthy. There are three practical reasons for eating by hand: .

1. Cleanliness — hands are naturally cleaner than any type of spoon as they are more often washed.

2. Digestion — hands crush food into smaller bites which enables proper chewing, which helps the digestion process. On the other hand, if you eat with fork or spoon you have to eat a big lumpy morsel, with another spoonful ready to eat even before you have finished chewing the first.

3. Spiritual Well-Being — the five fingers are representatives of the Panch Mahabhut or Five Elements: Air, Fire, Water, Earth and Ether. When these five elements join they become an entity of their own. So when five fingers enter the mouth with food, you are touching your own self (soul). This soothes and gives joy and satisfaction in eating.

As you eat do not take cold drinks in between the food as your fire is on and this does not help to digest the food. Take lukewarm drinks — especially clean water — which will prevent over-eating and help in digesting. After eating we normally take Pan or Mukhwas, which helps the digestive process and cleans the mouth and bad breath, bringing good aromas and creating more saliva which helps digestion.

And finally, after a meal Ayurveda says you must not sit or sleep but walk a few steps or stroll around, and then lie down on your left side for a few minutes as it helps the kidneys to process the food very easily and, again, helps to digest.

WHEAT

- Deepak is the standing oil lamp. It symbolises the dispelling of ignorance and awakening of the divine light within us. Its soft glow illuminates the temple or shrine room, keeping the atmosphere pure and serene.

WHEAT

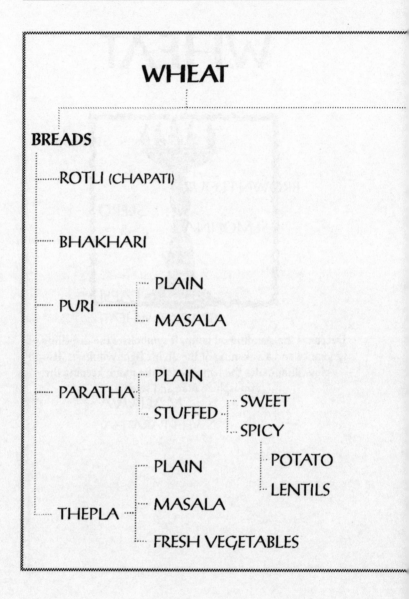

BREADS

ROTLI (CHAPATI)

BHAKHARI

PURI
- PLAIN
- MASALA

PARATHA
- PLAIN
- STUFFED
  - SWEET
  - SPICY
    - POTATO
    - LENTILS

THEPLA
- PLAIN
- MASALA
- FRESH VEGETABLES

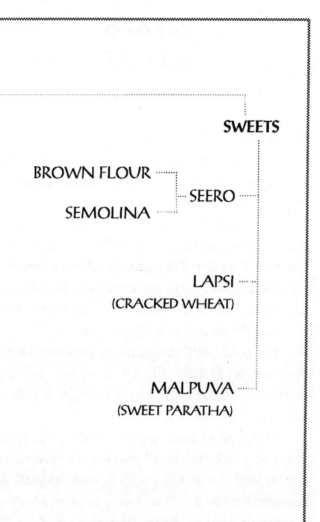

SWEETS

BROWN FLOUR
SEERO
SEMOLINA

LAPSI
(CRACKED WHEAT)

MALPUVA
(SWEET PARATHA)

61

BREADS

Introduction

The consistency of the dough is the most important factor in making any kind of bread, and varies according to whether you are making dough for chapati, puri or paratha.

The dough for puri should be drier and harder than that for chapati, the reason being that you will use more flour to roll the chapati (ataman), whereas for puri it is best not to use extra flour for rolling as the excess will drop off during deep-frying, burn and spoil the oil and subsequent puris.

For good health, chapatis are recommended as they are made from brown flour and are dry-roasted, whereas puris are deep-fried rendering them more difficult to digest.

The type of flour used is another important factor in successful bread-making. If very coarse flour is used (i.e. wholewheat) to make chapati, for example, the result will be a very hard bread which is more difficult to digest, and so a good quality 'atta' is used, i.e. 75% wholewheat flour.

MOVAN

This is the mixing of the right quantity of oil with the flour before water is added. In each case (chapati, puri, paratha, thepla, etc.) the "movan" will vary in quantity. Sometimes ghee (butter oil) is used in preference to oil, which alters the texture and taste of the finished item.

ATAMAN

This is the extra flour used in the rolling process; it must be used quickly and evenly and is kept in a separate tin or shallow bowl.

CHAPATI

This is the most popular of Indian breads. It is nourishing and healthy as, unlike some other breads, it is eaten immediately it is ready and should always be freshly made. It is not fermented and is very quick to make. It can be made from 75% wholemeal wheat flour and is dry-roasted on a flat pan, or griddle. It is normally rolled thinner than any other bread and is easily digested.

Ingredients
75% wholemeal wheat flour
any kind of oil or ghee
water, salt

Method
1. Put the flour in a small bowl and add a little oil. Mix well and add a little water to make a medium dough. Knead lightly with slightly oiled hands.
2. Divide the dough into, say, golf-ball size pieces (or break off individual amounts as you work) and roll out as thinly as possible, taking care to maintain a circular shape.

(The small round rolling platform used in India is called an 'adni' and the rolling pin 'lodhi (tavo)'.)

3. Pre-heat a griddle or any flat, heavy pan (in India this is called a 'tuvar') on a medium flame.

4. The chapati may be awkward to handle because it is so thinly rolled out. The best thing to do is to take it in the flat of the palm and slap it into the hot pan. Leave it to cook until small bumps appear on its surface (at this point the chapati is half cooked). Immediately turn it over. Cook until small golden to dark brown spots appear on its surface.

5. Remove pan from flame (or have another burner going) and place the chapati directly on to the flame first side (i.e. the half-cooked side) down.

6. The chapati should puff up with the heat; turn it quickly for a brief moment on to the other side and then place it on a flat dish or plate and spread with a little melted ghee.

(After much practice, the chapati can be turned using the hands, but until that time it is advisable to use a fork or tongs.)

Hints

To make a successful chapati takes patience and much practice. If you think the chapati is not cooked properly, it could be that the first side has been turned too soon. If it is overdone, or the dough was too hard, the chapati will not rise in the flame and will be hard. (The best way to learn correct chapati-making is to watch a demonstration by someone who knows!)

i)   When mixing the wholewheat flour and water, make sure that there is no flour left loose in the bowl and that the sides are completely clean.

ii)   After mixing the dough, lightly oil the hands and the whole lump of ready dough. This will ensure that when you remove a piece of dough for rolling it will not be sticky in the hand.

iii)   Generally, it is a good idea to make your dough half-an-hour before it is required. Do not use very cold or very hot water to make your dough — this will make the dough very sticky. Water should be room temperature.

iv)   The chapatis can be stacked one on top of the other on the serving plate.

BHAKRI

Another popular bread in India. It is nourishing, easily digested and usually eaten in the evening. It is like a chapati, only two or three times thicker.

Ingredients
90% or 100% wholewheat flour
oil or ghee
water, salt

Method
Similar to that for chapati, but the dough should be very solid and heavy, using more oil than in the chapati.

1.   When rolling out the dough, try not to use extra flour (which is why the dough should be firm and heavy). Make sure that the roller is more on the periphery of the dough so that an even circular shape is obtained. If the bhakri is unevenly rolled it will cook quicker in some areas than others , thus spoiling the finished item.

67

2. The bhakri is cooked in a flat heavy iron pan or griddle, on a slow to medium heat to ensure that the extra thickness is properly cooked. In all other respects it is cooked in the same manner as the chapati, leaving out the 'flashing' on the direct flame at the end. Spreading with ghee is optional.

3. This bread is slightly easier to make than chapati due to its thickness and easier rolling, so long as the dough is of the correct consistency.

PURI

This is yet another very popular bread all over India. Generally it is considered a rich man's bread because it needs deep oil for frying; it is light in appearance and taste. However, it is not as healthy as chapati or bhakri.

(The oil used for deep-frying can vary from pure ghee to any vegetable oil — according to taste, and pocket!)

Ingredients
75% wholewheat flour
oil
water, salt

Note: Do not use a flour stronger than 85% wholewheat, otherwise the puri will become too crisp in the cooking process and break.

Method
1. Prepare the dough. Its consistency should be firmer than that for chapati, but a little softer than that for bhakri. Take a small piece and roll it out thinly to about 3" in diameter (4" at the most). Do

not use extra flour for rolling out the dough.

2.   Heat the oil in a deep-frying pan (called a 'tavdi' in India). Be careful not to let the oil become too hot — with experience the flavour and texture of the finished puri will allow you to judge the correct temperature.

3.   Place the puri in the hot oil. If the temperature is correct the puri will puff-up into a ball and float on the surface of the oil. Leave it to cook for a little while (seconds only) and then turn it over.

Hints

The colour of the cooked puri should be a pale gold — it must not be allowed to brown.

The second side should be left to cook a little longer than the first. The reason being that one part of the puri will be thin and one part thick, and one must be sure to cook the thicker part properly. If the first side is cooked too much it will become brittle and break or crack open when the puri is turned over, allowing the hot oil to enter, spoiling the bread completely.

Generally, puris are soft. However, if you wish to make them crisp and eat them for breakfast, use full-strength wheat flour and make a firmer dough. Roll out the dough more thinly. When placed in the hot oil the puri will not puff-up and the finished item will be like a crisp biscuit.

If you wish to make a very special puri, you can use ghee for the 'movan', and milk instead of water to make the dough; deep-frying the puri in ghee. Once you have tasted these you will be in heaven!

MASALA PURI

The masala (spiced) puri is usually eaten for breakfast in India, or with afternoon tea. It is a very tasty puri and can be kept for a week or two without spoiling.

Ingredients
75% wholewheat flour
oil
water, salt
red or green chillies
fresh or dry ginger
haldi (turmeric) powder
small pinch of hing (asafoetida)

Method
1. Mix the the wholewheat flour thoroughly with the oil in a bowl; add the remaining ingredients; add enough water to make a firm dough.
2. Proceed as for the plain puri.

PARATHA
(plain)

This bread is very popular in Northern India. It is much heavier and thicker than the chapati and almost twice the thickness of bhakri, and very sustaining. Generally, in the north of India oil is not used in the making of the dough which results in a somewhat less soft and more 'rubbery' texture.

Ingredients
75% wholewheat flour
oil
water

Method
1. Make a firm dough as for the other breads.
2. Take a piece of dough (about twice or three times more than for the chapati), flatten it in the palm, make a small depression and add a little ghee or oil. Press the sides together and, after rolling it into a fat ribbon shape between the palms, make a 'swiss roll' shape. Stand this on end, flatten it and roll it out into a circular shape, not too thin.
3. Using a hot griddle or flat pan (as for the chapati), cook the first side. Turn the paratha over

73

and spread oil on the cooked side which is now facing you. Leave it to cook for a short time; turn it again, this time putting oil on the pan. Keep turning the paratha until it is cooked, but do not keep oiling the pan.

PARATHA
(stuffed)

This paratha can be made with various fillings — the most usual being potatoes or dals. The dough is made exactly the same as for a plain paratha, but it should not be too dry or hard or the filling will split out of the sides of the finished paratha.

POTATO FILLING

Boil and mash potatoes, making sure there are no lumps. To this you may add several ingredients according to taste), for example, a green masala with fresh green chillies and fresh ginger, or a dry masala with red chilli powder and garam masala and dry spices, or you can use both together if you wish. Fresh or dry garlic can also be added.

Method

1.   Take a small quantity or dough and flatten it. Take a small quantity or the filling and shape it into a ball. Wrap the dough around this ball of filling and press the sides together. Flatten the completed ball of dough and filling, and roll it out very carefully, seeing that the sides do not split.

2.   Cook in the same way as the plain paratha.

THEPLA
(plain)

This is another popular dish in Gujarat, and is eaten in the early morning and/or in the evening.

The dough is made in the same way as that for chapati.

Method

1. Take a small piece of dough and roll it out puri-size, not too thick. Spread a little oil on the surface; fold the rolled-out dough in half, spread a little oil on that side and fold. Roll out the dough until it is puri-size once more.

2. Cook on a hot griddle or heavy iron pan in the same way as that for paratha, until the bread is a dark golden colour. (Ghee may be used instead of oil.)

THEPLA
(masala)

The masala is similar to that used for the masala puri.

Method is the same as that for masala puri, but the dough is rolled out and folded and oiled in the same manner as the plain thepla.

THEPLA
(with fresh green leaf)

1. Add to the dough fresh chopped leaves of fenugreek (methi), coriander (dhania) or spinach.
2. Roll out and cook in the same way as the plain thepla.

ब्रह्मार्पणं ब्रह्म हविर्ब्रह्माग्नौ ब्रह्मणा हुतम् ।
ब्रह्मैव तेन गन्तव्यं ब्रह्मकर्मसमाधिना ॥

BRAHMĀ 'RPANAM BRAHMA HAVIR
BRAHMĀGNAU BRAHMANĀ HUTAM
BRAHMAI 'VA TENA GANTAVYAM
BRAHMAKARMASAMĀDHINĀ

For him the act of offering is God, the oblation is God.
By God is it offered into the fire of God.
God is that which is to be attained by him
who realizes God in his works.
—BHAGAVAD GITA

RICE

Kamal is the lotus flower, perfection of
beauty, associated with the deities and
the chakras, especially the 1,000-
petalled Sahasrara. Its blossom
promises purity and enlightenment.

RICE

- PLAIN

- BROWN

- PILAU

- VAGARELA (fried rice)

- BIRIYANI

- KHICHADI

- SWEET

PLAIN RICE

Preparation

Soak rice in room temperature water; the length of time will depend on the age of rice — the older the grain, the longer the soak.

Method

1. In a suitable pan bring fresh water to the boil and add rice — one handful each (if you are having bread etc.) or two if you are not. (The amount of water is generally $2^{1}/_{2}$ times the amount of rice, depending on how long it has been soaked and the age of the rice — experience will solve this question.)

2. Once the rice has started to boil do not add any extra water.

3. Lower heat and simmer very slowly until the grains have absorbed all the water. A spoonful of ghee may be added at this point and the rice left on a very low flame, or in a warm oven.

PLAIN BROWN RICE

Preparation
Soak overnight, with a little wholewheat if preferred.

Method
1.   Cook slowly with plenty of water (at least 3½ times water) on low flame.
2.   Add cinnamon and bayleaves before cooking.

PILAU RICE

Ingredients
rice (basmati preferably)
haldi powder _turmeric_
(or saffron,
either powdered or whole)
whole cinnamon stick
whole cardamoms and cloves
sliced cashews and almonds
bay leaves
whole jeera seeds _cumin_
oil
salt
water

Method

1. Put a little oil in pan and add a few cloves, the cinnamon stick, cardamoms, bay leaves. Cook until all the ingredients are a dark golden brown.

2. Add jeera seeds and immediately add rice; stir well and fry until the grain is slightly cooked. Add the haldi (or saffron) powder and mix well. Add nuts.

3. Add boiling water (three times the amount of

83

rice) and bring to the boil, reduce the flame to its lowest point, cover and cook until the grain has absorbed the water.

4.   Keep warm on a very low flame or in the oven.

VAGHARELA RICE

This dish is made from left-over rice (freshly cooked rice can of course be used if wished).

Ingredients
cooked rice
haldi powder
oil
jeera and dhania powders
rai seeds
methi seeds
fresh chopped dhania leaves
hing
fresh ginger and green chilli (or red chilli powder)

Method

VERSION 1
1.   Put a little oil in a pan, add cooked rice and stir. Add fresh crushed green chilli and ginger and haldi powder, jeera and dhania powders.
2.   In another pan fry methi seeds in about three spoonfuls of oil, when brown add rai seeds and cook until they crackle; add a pinch of hing.

3.   Add the prepared rice. Mix well over a medium heat and cook until the rice is heated through.

4.   Sprinkle with fresh chopped dhania leaves and cover.

VERSION 2

When frying methi and rai seeds, add thinly sliced garlic, fry until golden brown. Continue as for version 1.

VERSION 3

Add a squeeze of fresh lemon juice and some coconut during the final stage of cooking.

VERSION 4

After frying the rice, add buttermilk and simmer until it is absorbed.

VEGETABLE BIRYANI
(pilau)

= a vegetable dish with rice

Ingredients
rice
vegetables — any chopped
oil
jeera, methi *cumin* *fenugreek*
rai seeds *mustard*
fresh green chilli and ginger
haldi, jeera and dhania powders
turmeric *coriander*
hing
water and salt

Method
1. Wash rice and drain. Soak a little.
2. Put a little oil in a pan, add methi seeds and when browned add jeera and rai seeds, fry until they crackle.
3. Add a small pinch of hing.
4. Add rice and chopped vegetables, stir and cook for a further few minutes until rice is golden, stirring to prevent sticking.

87

5.   Add boiling water (about three times the amount of rice), haldi, jeera and dhania powders — salt to taste.

6.   Bring to the boil, lower heat, cover pan and simmer very slowly until all the water has been absorbed. Keep warm in the oven.

> The fear of cooking should go!
> You just do it, positively,
> and that's it.
>
> —RAMESH PATEL

KHICHADI*

This is a very nourishing dish made with rice and different dals (mung is the most popular) which is easily digested.

Ingredients
rice
dal (mung or tuvar)
haldi powder = turmeric (pinch)
water , pinch of salt

Note: if using mung dal: half rice and half dal; if using tuvar: three-quarter rice and one-quarter dal.

Method
1. Bring to the boil water two-and-a-half to three times the quantity of dry ingredients (if you require a more wet khichadi, four to four-and-a-half times as much water).
2. Add washed rice and dal.
3. Add a little haldi powder and salt, bring to boil, lower flame and simmer gently until grains are soft.
4. A spoonful of ghee can be added and the dish kept warm in the oven.

* For another version of this recipe, see Ayurvedic Meal for Two, page 147.

SWEET RICE

Ingredients
rice
cloves, cinnamon stick, whole cardamom
bay leaf
saffron
sugar (1 large spoon per person)
ghee
water
sultanas, cashew nuts

Method
1. Wash and drain rice.
2. Put a little ghee into a pan. In another pan keep some water boiling — say, two to two-and-a-half times the amount or rice — to which has been added sugar and saffron.
3. Add the cloves, cinnamon stick, whole cardamom to the ghee and fry until golden.
4. Add the rice, stir and cook until the rice has a little golden colour.
5. Add prepared sweetened water, bring to the boil, lower flame and simmer until the rice is soft — about seven minutes.

BEANS &
DALS

Ghanta is the bell used in ritual Puja. It engages not only the hearing but all the senses. Its ringing summons the Gods and reminds us that, like sound, the world may be perceived but not possessed.

BEANS

BEANS

- MUNG (Green Gram)

- MUTH

- CHANNA (Chickpeas)

- TUVAR (Pigeon Peas)

- URAD (Indian Black Gram)

- CHOLA (Blackeye beans)

- RAJMA (Red Kidney beans)

- BUTTER BEAN

- MIXED SPROUTED

DALS
(Split Pulses)

DALS

TUVAR (HARHAR DAL)

MASUR

MUNG

URAD (with or without skin)

TUVAR

Ingredients
tuvar dal
rai and methi seeds
whole dry red chillies
fresh green ginger and green chillies
tamarind soaked in a little water
jeera, dhania and haldi powders
garam masala
salt/sugar
hing
fresh green dhania

Method
1.   Boil the dal in plenty of water, until it is very soft (about 15 minutes).
2.   Pulp the soft dal using a whisk or egg-beater until a soup-like consistency is achieved. (The amount of water used for boiling the dal will of course dictate the consistency of the soup.)
3.   Add crushed green chilli and fresh ginger, tamarind, jeera, dhania and haldi powders, and garam masala. Bring soup to the boil, add salt and a little sugar if desired.

4. In another small pan fry methi seeds in a little oil until brown, add rai seeds and whole dry red chillies and cooked until dark brown. Add a pinch of hing.

5. Add this Vaghar to the soup (or vice versa) and observe the dramatic effect.

6. Cover and bring back to the boil on a high flame. Lower heat and simmer for about five minutes. Sprinkle with fresh dhania and serve with rice or as a soup.

VARIANT

Dates or peanuts may be added to the recipe, in which case cloves and cinnamon should be added to the Vaghar.

MASUR

This split pulse is cooked in the same way as tuvar dal.

MUNG DAL

This is prepared in more or less the same way as the tuvar, except that the garam masala and tamarind are omitted.

The vaghar may be varied by adding thin slices of garlic to the jeera, etc., seeds, adding lemon juice at the end for a slightly sour taste.

URAD DAL

This dal is prepared in the same way as the mung.

The vaghar is made with ghee rather than any other oil.

96

CHANNA

Ingredients
chickpeas
salt, turmeric
methi seeds
mustard seeds
garlic (chopped)
onion (chopped)
garam masala
green chili
lovage, hing
coriander, fenugreek

Method
1. Soak chickpeas overnight. Add salt and turmeric and cook in pressure cooker for ten minutes. (If not soaked, allow a further 5 minutes.)
2. Make a vaghar in a separate pan as follows: Put a little oil in the pan and add methi seeds, mustard seeds, chopped garlic, hing and lovage (together, to prevent burning) and onion (if desired: this is northern style, not used in Gujarat).
3. Add the garam masala, green chili, coriander, fenugreek, pinch of salt.

4. Stir and cook until a sauce is formed.

5. Add the chickpeas with their water. Cook slowly to let the seasonings take effect.

6. It can enhance the flavour to add a squeeze of lemon and a pinch of brown sugar.

Notes

1. Fenugreek, which is bitter, is added specifically to counteract the high degree of air present in channa.

2. Sugar is usually added with lemon to counterbalance the acid in the lemon.

CHOLA

Ingredients
blackeye beans
methi seeds
haldi
lovage
fenugreek
channa flour
turmeric
garam masala, salt

Method

1. Cook the beans in a pressure cooker for 10 minutes. Pour off the dark water.

2. Make a vaghar. Put some oil in a pan. Add methi seeds, haldi, lovage, fenugreek and stir in two small scoops of flour at the same time.

3. When the mixture starts to turn red, add the beans and some water. Simmer.

4. Add turmeric, garam masala, pinch of salt.

5. Put on a low heat and cover. Allow to cook for a few minutes.

6. Add a pinch of brown sugar to enhance flavour.

Note
Garlic and onion do not combine with chola, and for this reason we make a sauce with flour.

SAVOURIES & VEGETABLES

Vidya is Knowledge, Learning and Science. It is the true understanding that may be gained only through study and meditation. It is the lamp that guides us along the right path, removing the darkeness of ignorance, drawing us ever near the One.

SAVOURIES

SAVOURIES

GRAINS and VEGETABLES

- UPAMA

- IDLI

- HANDVO

- MUTHIA

- PATUDA

- SAMOSA

- DOSA

PULSES and VEGETABLES

- KACHARI

- DAL VADA

- BHAJIA

- PUDA

- DAHI VADA

- BATATA VADA

- PATRA

IDLI

Ingredients
rice
urad dal
salt

Method
1. Soak the rice and urad dal (2:1) for two or three hours (or until very soft). Grind to a coarse, thick paste and add salt and two spoonfuls of yoghurt.

2. Keep for a further 24 hours, at the end of which the paste will have fermented and will be very thick.

3. Put a little of the paste in each box of the idli pan and steam for 20 to 30 minutes.

HANDVO

Ingredients
rice
mung dal
tuva dal
fresh ginger, green chilli
haldi
red chilli powder (optional)
rai seeds
til seeds
whole dry red chillies
hing
yoghurt

Method
1. Soak rice, mung dal and tuva dal (1:½:½) in water until soft. Drain and grind to a paste. Add sufficient yoghurt to make a thick paste. Keep this overnight to ferment.

2. Add ground green masala (fresh ginger, green chilli), salt, and haldi; add red chilli powder if liked.

3. Put the paste in a non-stick pan and add two spoons of oil. Mix well.

4. In another small pan heat ½ cup of oil; add

105

dry red chillies, rai seeds and a pinch of hing. Remove pan from heat and immediately add 2 large spoonfuls of til seeds (sesame).

5.   Pour the mixture on top of the prepared paste.

6.   Place pan over moderate heat. Do not cover. Cook for at least half-an-hour.

7.   Serve hot or cold.

Note

Onion or marrow (dudhi) can be added if liked.

MUTHIA

Ingredients
wheat flour
chickpea flour (besan)
red chilli powder
haldi
dhania and jeera powder
green ginger and green chilli (ground)
oil
yoghurt
water

Method
1. Mix all the ingredients together to make a hard dough.
2. Roll the dough into a 'sausage' shape and steam it or fry it in a very little oil on a very low fire.
3. When it is cooked, slice it in small pieces and add a vaghar.

Note
Any vegetable may be added.

107

SAMOSA

Ingredients
chapati-type dough
potatoes
peas
cabbage
rai and methi seeds
hing
salt
chilli, jeera and dhania powders
garam masala
lemon and sugar (if desired)

Method
1. Boil the potatoes and chop into small pieces. Chop very fine carrots and cabbage.

2. Add a vaghar in sufficient oil of rai, methi and a pinch or hing. Add salt, chilli, jeera and dhania powders, and a little garam masala. Add potatoes and mix well.

3. Roll out the chapati dough thinly (white or wholemeal flour), into a small chapati, cut in two.

4. Place filling on one half and fold over to make a triangular shape. Fry in deep oil over a slow fire.

DOSA

Ingredients
rice flour
urad flour
salt
water

Method
1.   To rice and urad flours (3:1) add enough water to make a thin batter; add a pinch of salt. Add one or two spoonfuls of yoghurt. Leave overnight to ferment.

2.   Cook on a flat pan (tawa) as a thin pancake, spreading out the batter very quickly with the back of a spoon.

109

DAL VADA

Ingredients
channa or mung dal
onion
green ginger and green chilli
garlic
salt
haldi
oil
sodium bicarbonate

Method
1. Soak dal in water overnight. Crush to a coarse paste.
2. Add one small chopped onion, green ginger, green chilli, garlic, salt and haldi. Add a little oil and sodium bicarbonate. Mix well.
3. Make a small flat disc and fry in deep oil over a slow fire.

110

BHAJIA

Ingredients
besan
salt
haldi
red chilli powder
hing
sodium bicarbonate
oil
water
potatoes or onions or aubergines

Method
1. Add to besan, salt, haldi, red chilli powder, a pinch of hing and sodium bicarbonate.
2. Add a little oil and make a thin batter with water (add the water in a thin steady stream mixing all the while, to avoid lumps).
3. Slice thinly potatoes, onions, aubergines. Dip pieces in the batter and deep fry in hot oil for a short time.

Note
The bhajia can also be made with cauliflower, panir or even banana.

111

PUDA

PLAIN

Use the thin batter from the bhajia recipe. Pour on a flat oiled pan and fry in the same way as a dosa.

BLACKEYE BEAN

Ingredients
blackeye beans
salt
green chilli, green ginger
garlic (optional)
red chilli powder
haldi
oil

Method

1.   Soak the beans overnight. Grind to a paste and add crushed green chilli and ginger (garlic if used), chilli powder and haldi. Add a little oil.
2,   Add enough water to make a thin paste and fry with a flat pan in the same way as a dosa.

112

DAHI VADA

Ingredients
urad dal
mung dal, salt
green chilli and ginger
sodium bicarbonate
oil for deep frying
yoghurt
rai and jeera seeds
curry patra , ghee

Method

1.   Soak the dals overnight. Grind to a thick paste. Add salt ground green ginger and green chilli. Add a little sodium bicarbonate, mix well.

2.   Drop small balls of the paste into hot deep oil to cook until a pale gold colour (do not overcook). Remember the vada will swell to two or three times its size when cooked. Drain and put on one side.

3.   After draining the oil, put vadas in hot water or very thin buttermilk.

4.   Make the sauce by churning some yoghurt and adding a vaghar of rai and jeera seeds and a pinch of hing.

5.   Put the vadas into the dahi to soak well before serving.

113

BATATA VADA

Ingredients
besan
oil
salt
haldi
potatoes
salt
crushed green chilli and fresh ginger
garlic (optional)
haldi
hing
garam masala

Method
1, Boil and mash potatoes. Add salt, crushed green chilli and ginger and lemon crystals and sugar, and a little garam masala.
2, Mix well.
3, Make small balls and keep on one side.
4, Make a thin batter of the besan, a little oil, salt and haldi.
5, Dip the potato balls into the batter and deep fry briefly.

114

PATRA

Ingredients
besan
imli (tamarind)
sugar
patra (special green leaf)

Method
1, Make a thick batter with the besan, similar to that for bhajia, add a paste of imli and sugar.

2, Take fresh patra, wash and dry then spread the batter very thinly over its surface. Place two or three leaves on top of each other (batter side to underside of leaf in each case); fold the sides so that it is a rectangular shape and then roll it up so that it looks like a fat cigar. Steam until it is cooked.

3, To serve, cut the roll into thin slices. Add a vaghar of rai, garlic and hing.

Note
You can use large spinach leaves instead of patra leaves.

115

KACHORI

Ingredients
mung dal
garam masala
star aniseed powder (pinch)
haldi, turmeric
salt, lemon crystals
sugar, raisins
flour, oil

Method
1. Boil the mung dal until it is just a little bit hard. Drain the water.
2. Add garam masala, star aniseed powder, salt, haldi and turmeric.
3. Add sugar and lemon crystals, and raisins (optional)
4. Make a dough. Take some scoops of flour and add a generous amount of oil (to make a crisp dough when fried). Very little water may be added.
5. Roll out the dough and fill with the mixture. Make small sealed parcels.
6. Deep fry, allowing time for the dough to cook and become crisp and golden.

116

FRESH MANGO CURRY

Ingredients

Alfonso mango
caripata leaves
cinnamon, cardamom
cloves
oil
fenugreek, mustard seeds
hing, cumin
coriander, garam masala
turmeric, salt
ginger, green chili

Method

1. Cut the mango into 4 pieces.
2. Heat a little oil in a pan and add caripata leaves, cinnamon, cardamom and cloves.
3. Add fenugreek, mustard seed and a pinch of hing.
4. Throw in the mango pieces and cover immediately to preserve the vaghar.
5. Add water to cover the mango and cover again.

6. Add remaining spices.

7. When the mango is soft and the skin is coming off, it is ready. This normally takes about 10 to 15 minutes.

Notes

1. The Alfonso mango has smooth flesh, rather than threads, and is therefore the correct type to use.

2. This dish may be eaten with bread or rice. If rice is chosen, allow a little more liquid to remain at the end of cooking.

118

DUDHI

Ingredients
marrow (thin, whitish
type)
oil
fenugreek, mustard seeds
asafoetida
mustard powder
salt, cumin
coriander, garam masala
green chili
garlic
brown sugar

Method
1.   Slice the marrow into quarter pieces
2.   Heat a little oil in a pan (one with a lid). Add fenugreek, mustard seed, asafoetida.
3.   Add marrow, and then the mustard powder, salt, cumin, coriander and garam masala.
4.   Cover and put on a slow flame for 15 or 20 minutes.
5.   Towards the end, add a little green chili and garlic, and a pinch of brown sugar.

119

Note

1. Fenugreek reduces the air quality of the marrow, and the mustard seed raises the fire element, while asafoetida takes out excess air through the stomach. This is the vaghar designed to balance with the marrow.

POTATO AND ONION CURRY*

Ingredients
potato
onion
fenugreek
mustard seed
hing, turmeric
garam masala
green chili–garlic mix
paprika
sugar, lemon

Method

1. Cut the potato and onion into small squares.
2. Make a vaghar of fenugreek, mustard seed and hing.
3. Add the vegetables and keep cooking.
4. Add the turmeric and garam masala, and a little green chili and garlic mix.
5. If the colour becomes flat, add some paprika powder.
6. Add a little sugar and lemon just at the end.

---

* For another version of this recipe, see Ayurvedic Meal for Two, page 149.

अन्नाद्भवन्ति भूतानि पर्जन्यादन्नसम्भवः
यज्ञाद्भवति पर्जन्यो यज्ञः कर्मसमुद्भवः

ANNĀD BHAVANTI BHUTĀNI
PARJANYĀD ANNASAMBHAVAH
YAJNĀD BHAVATI PARJANYO
YAJNAH KARMASAMUDBHAVAH

From food come forth beings,
from rain food is produced,
from Yajna, the fruit of your deeds, arises rain,
and Yajna is born of Karma.

SWEETS

Go, the Cow, is a symbol of the earth, the nourisher, the ever-giving, undemanding provider. In Hinduism, all animals are sacred, and this reverence of life finds acknowledgement in special affection for the gentle cow.

SWEETS

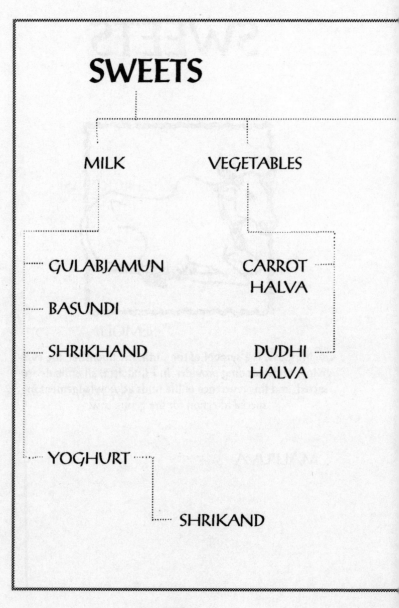

MILK

VEGETABLES

GULABJAMUN

CARROT
HALVA

BASUNDI

SHRIKHAND

DUDHI
HALVA

YOGHURT

SHRIKAND

124

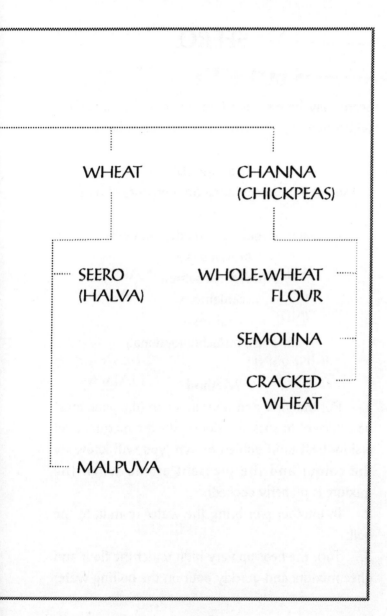

WHEAT

CHANNA
(CHICKPEAS)

SEERO
(HALVA)

WHOLE-WHEAT
FLOUR

SEMOLINA

CRACKED
WHEAT

MALPUVA

SEERO

Seero may be prepared from 85% or 100% whole-wheat flour, or semolina, or a mixture of both.

Ingredients
Wheat flour or semolina (or a mixture of both)
ghee
water or milk (or a mixture of both)
brown sugar
powdered saffron
cardamom
raisins
almonds, pistachio (optional)

Method
1.   Put the ghee and flour in a pan (the ghee must be sufficient to soak the flour). Stir the mixture over a slow heat until golden brown (you will know by the colour and the pleasant aroma when the mixture is properly cooked).
2.   In another pan bring the water or milk to the boil.
3.   Turn the heat up very high under the flour and ghee mixture and quickly pour on the boiling water

or milk and stir continuously (the amount of fluid to aim at is two-and-a-half times the amount of flour and ghee mixture, but if the flour is very rough more fluid may be required). The combined ingredients will bubble furiously. Keep stirring the mixture over a high heat until the fluid has been absorbed. Lower the heat and simmer until the seera is firm.

4. Add brown sugar, according to taste, and cardomom, almonds, raisins and nuts. Stir and simmer for a little longer because the heat will release the water from the sugar and it is necessary to cook this out of the seero so that it is quite 'dry'.

Note

Generally, in India sweets are prepared only with pure ghee as it is a light, sweet tasting oil.

LAPSI

This is prepared from cracked wheat in a similar manner to seera.

Ingredients
cracked wheat
ghee
water (4 or 5 times the quantity of cracked wheat)
brown sugar
cardamom
raisins

Method
1. As for seera, cook the cracked wheat over a slow heat with the ghee, until golden brown (once again you will notice the pleasant aroma).
2. Add enough boiling water to cover the wheat and bring the mixture to simmering point. Cover and simmer until the wheat has absorbed all the water.
3. Add sugar, cardamom and raisins and cook until all fluid has been absorbed.

MALPUVA
(sweet paratha)

This sweet paratha is a very rich dish, eaten on special and festive occasions.

Ingredients
85% wholemeal flour
ghee
water (4 or 5 times the amount of flour)
whole black peppercorns
yoghurt, sugar

Method
1.   Add sugar (according to taste) to the water and bring to boil, stir until the sugar melts and a clear very light syrup is formed. Let it cool.
2.   In a large pan combine the sweet water with a large spoonful of flour and mix thoroughly with your hand, using a circular motion.
3.   To this add the rest of the flour, a little yoghurt and black peppercorns. The result should be quite a fluid batter and this is left to ferment overnight.

To cook
1.   Pour ghee into a steel frying pan to a depth of

129

about 1$\frac{1}{2}$" and bring it to a simmering point.

2. Take a small ladle of the mixture and pour it quickly into the oil with a circular motion. Fry for a few minutes until golden brown, turn it over and cook the other side.

BASUNDI

Ingredients
full cream milk
sugar
cardamom
pistachio nuts and almonds (ground
saffron powder

Method
1,   Bring milk to boil and simmer until it thickens. Stir frequently to prevent milk solids sticking to the bottom of the pan and burning.
2,   Add sugar, cardamom and chopped nuts, with a little saffron.

SHRIKAND

Ingredients
yoghurt
saffron and cardamom powder
sugar

Method
1,   Hang the yoghurt in a muslin cloth to remove the water for at least one or two days.
2,   This should then be placed over the top of an empty pan, the ends drawn together and tied with string.
3,   When all the fluid has dripped out, add sugar and mix well. If possible, sieve through a cloth, add saffron and cardamom and serve.

CARROT HALVA

Ingredients
carrots
ghee
milk
sugar
cardamom powder and saffron if you want

Method
1,   Grate carrots finely and fry gently in ghee until soft and dry without water. Add plenty of milk and bring mixture to the boil. Simmer until the milk has thickened. Stir constantly. Add sugar. Continue to simmer until it thickens.

2,   When the mixture is very thick, add cardamom powder and saffron.

3,   Can be served hot or cold.

Note
Dudhi (Indian marrow) halva is made in the same manner, substituting marrow for the carrots.

YOGHURT

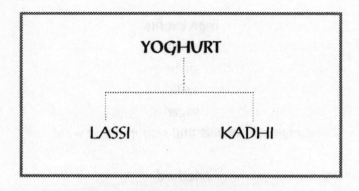

```
              YOGHURT
                 |
        .........|.........
        :                 :
      LASSI             KADHI
```

Chandra is the Moon, ruler of the watery realms and of
emotion, testing place of migrating souls. Surya is the Sun,
ruler of intellect, source of truth. One is Pingala and lights the
day, the other is Ida and lights the night.

HOW TO MAKE YOGHURT

1. Bring some milk to the boil; let it cool to room temperature and add two spoonfuls of yoghurt, mix well.

2. Keep container covered in a warm place overnight. The yoghurt will be ready when the milk has set in the morning.

LASSI

Add water to yoghurt and blend well, either by hand with an egg-beater or in an electric mixer.

SWEET

Add brown sugar or honey. Add mango pulp for Mango Lassi.

SALT

Add salt and cumin powder. (Dry roast the cumin seeds before grinding.)

135

KADHI*

Ingredients
lassi
besan
salt
haldi
chopped green ginger and green chilli
jeera seeds, cloves
hing
curry patra
ghee

Method
1. Add two tablespoons of besan to some lassi (make a thin batter first with some of the lassi). Mix well and add salt, haldi, chopped ginger and chilli. Bring mixture to the boil and simmer for over half-an-hour.

2. If the yoghurt is sour then add gur (jaggari or brown sugar) to taste.

3. Add a vaghar of ghee with jeera seeds, a few cloves, hing and curry patra (sweet neem leaves). Cook for a little while longer and serve.

* For another version of this recipe, see Ayurvedic Meal for Two, page 148.

136

RAITA

VARIANT 1
Grate finely cucumber and carrots. Add to yoghurt. Add salt, a little sugar and a vaghar of ghee with jeera and rai seeds and a pinch of hing.

VARIANT 2
Add a sliced banana to yoghurt. Add salt, a little sugar and a little mustard powder and vaghar.

VARIANT 3
Add chopped boiled potato to yoghurt. Add salt, a little brown sugar, mustard powder and vaghar.

VARIANT 4
Add chopped onion and boiled potato, then add salt, brown sugar and mustard powder and add vaghar.

CHUTNEYS

Shatkona is a star made of two interlocking triangles. The
upper is Shiva, Purusha and Fire, the lower is Shakti, Prakriti
and Water. Their union gives birth to Sanatkumara, whose
sacred number is six.

DHANIA CHUTNEY

In a blender put chopped green dhania, green chillies, fresh ginger, a little sugar, lemon juice and two spoonfuls of til seeds. Blend well.

COCONUT CHUTNEY

1. In a blender put some grated coconut, peanuts, a spoonful of til seeds, whole jeera and green chillies. Blend well.
2. If too thick, add yoghurt or water. However, this is not necessary.
3. Add a vaghar of ghee with jeera and rai seeds, hing and curry patra.

THREE DAY CLEANSING ROUTINE

Naga, the Cobra, is a symbol of Kundalini power, cosmic energy coiled and slumbering within man. It inspires seekers to overcome misdeeds and suffering by raising the power of the serpent up the spine into God-Realization.

अन्नं ब्रह्म

ANNAM BRAHMA

Food is God.

DAY ONE

A liquid fast. Needless to say, this does not include alcohol. Begin the day with a glass of fresh orange juice with black pepper and a bit of salt: citrus clears the taste, salt helps restore the taste to the tongue and black pepper aids digestion and clears mucus from the body. For the rest of the day, only water, juice, tea and the liquid from cooking mung beans (dal).

DAY TWO

V ery light food such as boiled vegetables, thick soups and bread, which will give energy and relieve bodily heaviness. Avoid meats and dairy products. An ideal Ayurvedic meal is rice and mung dal, yoghurt soup, and potato and onion curry (see next section).

DAY THREE

S tick with the Ayurvedic meal. You might also include green salads, fresh fruit salads, brown flour bread or chappatis. Continue to avoid refined or commercially prepared foods, as well as meat and dairy products.

Kamandalu, the water vessel is carried by the Hindu
monastic. It symbolizes his simple self-contained life, his
freedom from wordly needs, his constant Sadhana and Tapas,
and his oath to seek God in every part.

AYURVEDIC MEAL FOR TWO

This consists of **khichadi** (rice and mung dal),
kadhi (yoghurt soup), and potato and onion curry.
The entire meal can be prepared in 30 minutes.
Start with khichadi, then do the kadhi, and finally
the potato and onion curry.

Anjali is the gesture of two hands pressed together and held near the heart. It is the traditional Hindu greeting, signifying the intention to celebrate and honour — two joined as one, the bringing together of matter and spirit, the self meeting the Self.

KHICHADI

1. Take 2 handfuls of rice and one handful of mung dal and wash well. Put in a covered pot and add water to almost one inch above the rice/dal mixture.

2. Add a pinch or two of salt, and 2 to 3 pinches of turmeric. Let simmer on slow flame, covered, for 15-18 minutes.

KADHI

1. Mix a small part of yoghurt in a bowl with 2 parts of water to 1 part of yoghurt and mix well.

2. Add one small handful of gram flour (chick pea flour) and mix well: this keeps the yoghurt from splitting.

3. Add 2 pinches of salt, a big pinch of turmeric and chopped green chillies and chopped ginger to taste. Have ready cumin seeds, asafoetida, curry leaves, ghee and whole cloves.

4. To a pot on low heat add one spoon of ghee, 3 to 4 cloves, 5 to 6 curry leaves and, when hot, add a big pinch of cumin seeds which will pop immediately, then add a pinch of asafoetida.

5. With a cover for the sauce pot in one hand, take the yoghurt mixture in the other and put into the hot pot. Cover immediately.

6. Allow to cook on slow flame for 15 to 20 minutes, stirring to prevent it from boiling over. Taste and, if the yoghurt is very sour, add a pinch of sugar.

148

POTATO AND ONION CURRY

1. Take 2 to 3 small potatoes (or one large potato) and one or two small onions (or half a Spanish onion), peel and chop into large pieces and keep separate.

2. Have ready asafoetida, methi seeds, mustard seeds, turmeric, salt, powdered cumin, powdered coriander, chopped fresh green chillies and ginger. Put a pan on a slow flame and add a bit of oil, add a pinch of fenugreek (methi) seeds and before it changes colour too much to reddish add a pinch of mustard seeds which will immediatey start to pop, and add a pinch of asafoetida. Take a fistful of potato and put into pan and cover immediately.

3. Add the rest of the potato and cover. After a few seconds pour water over to cover.

4. When potatoes are half cooked, add onion, 2 to 3 pinches of turmeric, 2 to 3 pinches of salt, 2 to 3 pinches of cumin and 2 to 3 pinches of coriander. Cover again and let cook until onion is soft.

5. Add fresh ginger and chilli.

Optional

You can also add paprika or chilli powder near the end of cooking and/or fresh tomato, tomato puree — or even tomato ketchup — and a pinch of brown sugar.

---

10 DO NOTS...

1. DO NOT USE tinned food

2. DO NOT USE food with preservatives

3. DO NOT USE food colouring

4. DO NOT USE artificial flavouring

5. DO NOT USE white sugar

6. DO NOT USE white flour

7. DO NOT USE white rice

8. DO NOT USE margarine

9. DO NOT USE microwave ovens

10. DO NOT USE cold or stale food

INDEX OF DISHES

ईशावास्योपनिषद्
शान्तिपाठ

ॐ पूर्णमदः पूर्णमिदं पूर्णात् पूर्णमुदच्यते
पूर्णस्य पूर्णमादाय पूर्णमेवावशिष्यते

ॐ शान्तिः शान्तिः शान्तिः

INVOCATION

PURNAM ADAH, PURNAM IDAM, PURNĀT
PURNAM UDACHYATE PURNASYA PURNAM
ĀDĀYA PURNAM EVĀVASISYATE

That is full, this is full. The full comes out of the full:
Taking the full from the full the full itself remains.
AUM, peace, peace, peace.
—ISA UPANISAD

The Wheel, Chakra, represents the circle of time, the symbol
of perfect creation, of the cycles of existence. Time and space
are interwoven, and its spokes mark the directions, each ruled
by a Deity and having a unique quality.
AUM.

ॐ श्रीपरमात्मने नमः